MiXED
FEELiNgs

MIXED FEELINGS

AVAN JOGIA

POEMS AND STORIES

Andrews McMeel
PUBLISHING®

Introduction.

Mixed Feelings started like a storm,
a swirling of ideas that began to take shape,
the eye of which was always unseeable to me
and will most likely remain unseeable until this book is finished.

I have always felt out of place in this world.
A world, it seems, that is increasingly polarised.

By RACE
By Gender
By Sexuality
By Religion
By Politics

By anything anyone can use as a vehicle of division.
People are taking a stand on "their" side of the line
and seeing their enemies in the faces of those on the other side.

But I know something that they might not know.
And so do all people who share a mixed upbringing
or hold within them the currents
of seemingly opposed forces.

What we know
is that there is no line.
Matrix shit. There is no spoon.

But that's Not how this Book Started

When it started, I was using only my eyes to see what being mixed meant. My race. My two halves. But after listening to all of you speak about what your eyes see, it became clear to me that this is bigger than any one vehicle of division.

The parts don't add up to the sum.

I discovered that the further out you zoom on that feeling of "mixedness," the more it includes everyone.

Now, this isn't meant to be revelatory.
I'm sure most of you are saying, "Well, fuck, duh . . ."
But I would be inflating my intellect if I was to pretend
that it didn't hit me sideways as I crossed the street.

HiT & RuN

Concussed by this idea,
I kept zooming out and zooming out
until I felt what can only be described as the feeling
astronauts get on their first spaceflight.
That overhead feeling.
And I saw how truly connected we all are.
And I saw, as most astronauts do,
how truly vulnerable we all are,
floating in the middle of nothing.

So that's what this book is meant to do. It's meant to
produce that societal overhead feeling. After writing this,
I don't see the lines that divide us in the same way, and if
that is the single thing this book achieves, I'll mark it as a
success.

But again, the storm.

I see the swirling of hundreds of millions of people who feel
the same way I do.
Who are, like me, unsatisfied with these vehicles of division
and how they are used to separate us.

If you are like me, you understand how complicated these
titles can be.

Race.
Gender.
Sexuality.
Religion.
Politics.

You understand that these titles belong to your "mixed bag of motivations," and that your identity can be motivated by all of them at once, or none of them at all.

Mixed Feelings
        is a
          ·StorM SONg·

It's about the swirling of ideas.
These are just mine, spilling from my own mixed bag of motivations.
And I hope, with some luck, they give you that overhead feeling.
I hope you, after reading this book,
feel inclined to spill your bag on the world.

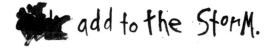 add to the StorM.

A, Boy can DrEam.

                    — AVAN

Mohammed Omar Atif

Mohammed's parents met in the summer of
1981 in his father's cab.

His father had been sleeping on park benches in New York.
He had come from Kuwait City and was trying to find
his uncle, who he eventually found, and who passed away
just last year.

His mother
was from the Dominican Republic,
and she lived in Washington Heights
with her whole family.
Which is where Mohammed's father was taking her
when they met.
The meter ran and ran
and so did their mouths
so they turned off the meter
and they circled the block for a while
and have been circling each other ever since.

Mohammed was born in New York three years before 9/11
and lost his front teeth being beaten and called a terrorist
several years later.

"I just forgave everyone I hated," he says.
Mohammed has kind eyes and a soft voice.

His parents changed Mohammed's name to
Omar after the towers fell.

Priya Peña

My parents met in a poetry class. They almost didn't get married. My mother is Hindu and my father is Christian. So that was the bigger conflict than race, although my grandfather on my dad's side called my dad when my brother was first born and asked what color his skin was.

do you have the "good" Mix?

they ask.
Do you have the "good" mix?

(Insert Lighter SKIN)

I have the good MIX.

I say to myself.

I have my father's grace
and my mother's fire and wit.
I have my father's eyes
and my mother's smile.

I have the "good" mix.

and so do you.

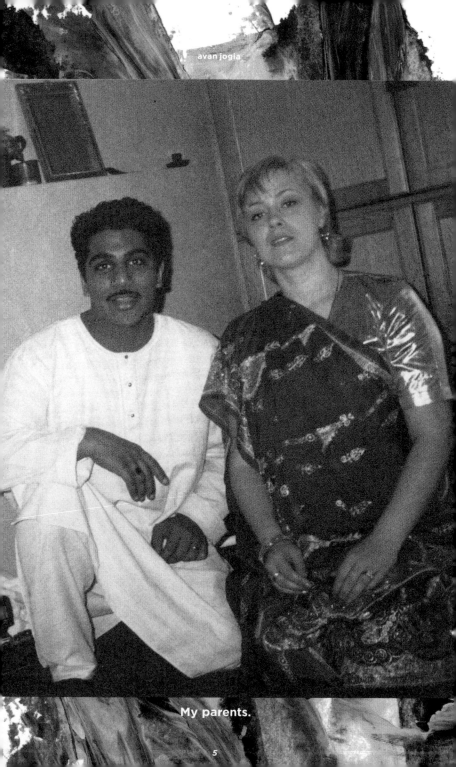

avan jogia

My parents.

Teaching Time.

My father gave me his gold watch
from the family safe
and it shines
reminding me of who I am:
The son of a jeweller.
The son of the man who taught me patience,
who taught me time.

I used to be in such a hurry
and I still am
from time to time.
My father told me,
"Don't rush, don't worry."
I'll get what I want
if it's meant to be mine.

My father's gold watch tells me
it will all come in due time.

Third-Culture Kid

The Third-Culture Kid snakes her way down the street
you can't stop her walking she's a rare fucking beast
her hair is all cut off and she's riding a ram.

Right on, Uncle Sam!

The Third-Culture Kid is a road poem.
The Third-Culture Kid is the lamb.
The Third-Culture Kid is exactly as I am.

Hot damn!

Here she comes in her newspaper dress and the headline
reads
"Third-Culture Kid Named President for Life in Landslide
Election!"
Third-Culture Kid is commander in chief
and she feels all right.

Right on, Uncle Sam!

The Third-Culture Kid is a road poem.
The Third-Culture Kid is a brand.

Trayvon R.I.P.

Eric R.I.P.

Tamir R.I.P.

Philando R.I.P

Kilala Vincent

My background is Japanese and African American. I was around my mother, who is Japanese, all the time. I immersed myself in Japanese culture and spoke Japanese as often as I could. Early in my life, I knew that I wanted to be just like her.

I was sitting in the car with my father one day, driving back home, when I told him I wanted to be just like my mom. I told him that I was now "only Japanese." Although it was a joke, my father was hurt and angry. He turned around to look at me and began to yell, telling me that not only would I never be Japanese, but no one would ever see me as Japanese, let alone mixed.

I was beyond crushed. I was in over my head. I knew I had better get my act together because the world was cruel and would not let a girl like me continue such fantasies. For a long time, I didn't understand what my father had meant. I began to question what I was and assumed that everyone had the same self-critical thoughts that I had. I avoided going to Japanese school in fear that I would get teased or be called a fraud. I felt a sort of anger toward both my black side and my father who constantly lectured me about being black in America—a concept I was already beginning to hate.

In 2012, Trayvon Martin was murdered by George Zimmerman. In 2014, Eric Garner was choked to death by a Staten Island police officer. In the same year, Tamir Rice, a twelve-year-old boy, was shot to death while playing in a park. In 2016, Philando Castile was shot four times in front of his family. The list goes on. It became clear to me, shooting after shooting, that I was a target. So were my father and six-year-old sister. So were my aunts, uncles, and cousins. So were my friends, and any other black person who happened to be at the wrong place at the wrong time.

The words my father had said to me began to click. I stopped avoiding articles on black history and began to read. I stopped distancing myself from black culture and instead embraced it as much as I did my Japanese culture. In doing so, I learned to love the influences of both my father and my mother.

My First Friend.

My First Friend, My Brother.

For the first two years, I didn't even speak.
I didn't have to.

You would make sure I got the same as you.

I still look at you
the way I look at you in this photo.
You taught me and still teach me.
We are in life together.
We discovered what being a person was about together
and through our teenage years, and all the new,
I had someone who I could turn to.

Our father and his brother
drink port in our living room,
listening to their dub tapes from England.
Sugar Minott's "Good Thing Going."
Retelling their stories.

I can't wait to do that with you.

My brother.
My partner.
My first friend.

I love you.

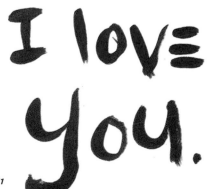

I love you.

My First Home.

I was born in government housing
apartments stacked on top of each other.

Concrete slab fencing made from repurposed construction
materials that my brother and I used to climb like the walls
of some medieval castle.

We lived in the bottom basement unit
beneath my mother's parents and
my father's parents
lived in a unit down the street.

I remember the feeling of linoleum floor on my bare feet.
Cheap, sticky, plastic sheets.
And beige carpets.

My head still bears the scars from metal bracers
laid underneath cheap drywall corners that I would run into
while playing with my brother.

Mum's Tree.

I can't recall if our bedroom had a window
but we had a bunk bed
and my mother had painted a tree on the wall.

I was born in government housing
apartments stacked on top of each other.

Packed so tight, I can still feel the closeness.

COLOURED CHILD!

I am the brown man picking up cans
getting accosted by an officer
making demands
      "Show me your hands!"
Show me your badge!
        "Obey my commands!"
What am I doing wrong, officer?
I don't understand.

Bam.

I am the black woman hugging her kids
getting assaulted by an officer
"Where do you live?
(A punch in the ribs)
"Answer me! Those aren't your kids."
Why are you doing this, officer?
I just want to live.

Damn.

I am the brown woman in a hijab
getting confronted by her coworker
losing her job.
"Take that shit off!
You heard me right.
Take that shit off!
You want to live here?
You have to respect American laws."

Man.

I am the coloured child, not allowed to run wild,
can't get angry, 'cause that anger just might
get me profiled.
This same wise child
smiled after being reviled
because his beauty was so beguiling
it could not be defiled.

SP=AK YOUR BloodLIN=

They talk about you in a language you understand, laughing at jokes that you know are about you.
Just because your face doesn't look like your voice sounds.

So when you open up your mouth to speak,

They h=AR YOUR BloodLIN=

The little bald boy knows what's true.

The Bald Boy.

In this photo, I look so sure.

And I haven't been this sure since.
As I get older, I have to remind myself
who I am
over and over.

"Be the little bald boy in the photo, old chap."
"Have some grace and be bolder."

But I guess that's what happens
as you get older.
You forget why you got pulled

mixed feelings

from the wheel in the first place
to inhabit this form
and take on this life.

"Be the little bald boy in the photo, old chap."
"Practice forgiveness."
"Live not in strife."

And as you grow and grow,
it seems that the things you know
pull you farther and farther from truth.
Like an ache in your tooth
or a stone in your boot.
A small pain that you learn to live around.

Painful uncertainty over what is fundamentally you.

But remember:
The little bald boy knows what is true.
And that means you do too.

avan jogia

My Balmo Vara.

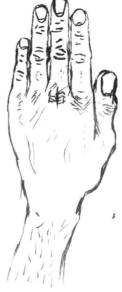

My Balmovara.

I remember my Ba's hands
mostly.
Soft and strong as she cracked
her knuckles on her head for
luck.

A blessing.

I remember sitting on a stool
in our tiny, low-rent apartment living room
jam-packed with my relatives who had come
from all over the world to see me.

"Okay," my mother said warmly. "Say 'bye-bye, hair.'"
"Bye-bye, hair!" I exclaimed, smiling,
happy to be the center of attention.

Buzzzzzzzzzz.

I remember the hum of the clippers
vibrating over my head as my hair,
which had been uncut since birth,
was shaved off.

I think that outside America, I am just a person. While race is observed or inferred, it's not usually a topic of conversation and I am able to just exist.

Observed and inferred.

We aren't asking you to
keep yourself from thinking,
"I wonder where this person is from."

We get that.
It's natural.
Fuck, I do it all the time.

We are asking you to stop
making your curiosity
our problem.

Sarinah Pond

That's when it's exhausting.
I just want to exist.
Sometimes I haven't the
patience to be a fucking historian.
Sometimes I just want to exist.

It's like asking a woman if
she's pregnant.
You could get it right.
But if you're wrong,
it's going to be uncomfortable.
It's better to just observe and infer.

BECAUSE She is "Just White"

At family gatherings, she has to prove
she knows the food
and the culture
and the dance.

Elders wait to reprimand her
for the whiteness
in the way she speaks or
in her stance.

She is "just white."

When she talks about her ancestry
in mixed company
she has to bear the looks of
"Who does this white girl think she is?"
As if she doesn't belong to them,
her own culture, mixed and muddy.
As if she's not as strong as them.
As if her bloodline isn't as long as them.

Oh, how we make people feel "other!"
We don't see sisters, fathers, brothers, mothers.
We see "just white."

When my uncle got married in a big, blowout Indian wedding, I wore my lehenga and chuni and felt like I was playing dress-up. It was custom-made for me, but it didn't feel like it really fit me, and I know that I only felt beautiful in it because I felt exotic.

My uncle tells his children to call me "Fionaben," adding a suffix that means "sister," but it feels funny to add "ben" to a name that isn't Indian.

Sometimes I feel inauthentic in my quests to understand my Indian heritage. Sometimes I don't feel like I should be allowed to eat shaak and rotli and rice and daal with my right hand, even though that is how I ate those meals with my grandmother. Or to wear a sari to a wedding and take a picture of myself because I look nice. Or to say that I am Indian when I don't look it, and my connection to my family feels faint and far away.

I had to look up how to spell some names of foods to write this e-mail. Just mentioning them makes me feel inauthentic, even though I grew up eating shaak and rotli and rice and daal.

I often feel jealous of mixed kids who look more mixed. I think that if I looked more Indian, I would feel more connected to being Indian, and I wonder why I am drawn to wanting to be closer to that part of me.

Fiona Brackley

Mixed Feelings.

I find it hard to write about my race
because my feelings are written on my face.
Not in my expression,
but in the peaks of my nose
and the valleys of my sunken eyes.

White nose.
Brown eyes.
Mixed feelings.

Choose a side.
I can't.
I'm unable.

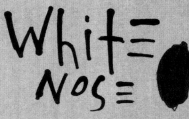

What is written on my face is the answer.
It is woven into the tapestry of my DNA.

To all the
Indian-Irish
Jamaican-Scottish
Filipino-Italian
Icelandic-Chinese
Korean-Ghanaians

I won't let them make us pick a side.
I'd rather be a mixed being
with mixed feelings.

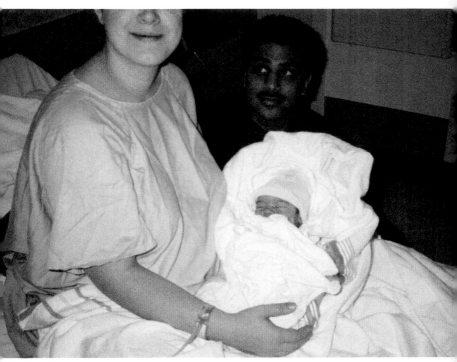

The day I was born.

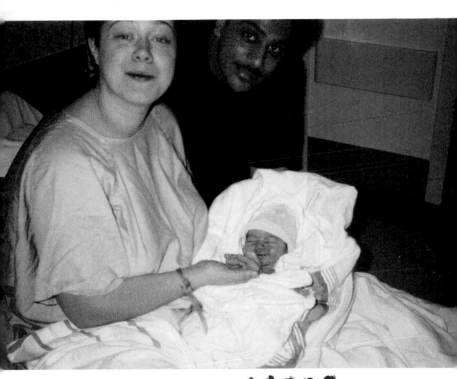

Feb 9th 1992

My naME is not
That hard to
Be Fucking
pronounce

Sorry, Susan.

My name is not that hard to fucking pronounce.
I'm tired of hearing otherwise.
And I'm sure you've heard it too.
All the Aidas Habibs Hamadis Zhongs Priyas
You get it.

Do you know how many times I've sat there
having said and re-said it,
a smile tacked on my face as I listen
to someone try to introduce me?

All you have to do is ask,
"How do I say your name again?"
That's it.

Instead I have to hear you
bastardise my name in ways
that are frankly impressive. Avon A Van Evan

"It's Gavin without the G," I could say.
But I'm tired of making it easy for you.

Although, if I am honest,
I spend so much time explaining my name,
I rarely catch yours. Sorry Susan, I think

Kiere Doherty JAMES

Kiere's mother was born on the rocky shores
of Ireland and came to the eastern coast of America
where she met Kiere's father,
an immigrant himself
from the warm sands of Trinidad
who came to that same eastern coast
to study at Columbia University
on a scholarship.

Trinidad
is the most mixed place
I've ever been.
The warm beaches melt
seamlessly into warm faces
and I can take deep breaths
of comfort and calm
having, for once in my life,
not been made to feel different
or other
or exotic.

I've been called exotic more times than I can count and approached in languages I can't name, let alone understand.

New York City
is the second-most mixed place
I've ever been.

But there
it is different.
America is there
leaning its weight on everything,
asking you all the questions, you,
being made to feel different
or other
or exotic.

No identity
No different
No other
No exotic

But I felt, and continue to feel, free in that I can be unidentifiable.

Autumn–Myst

After my parents married, they settled in Montreal, Quebec, Canada. As a kid, I always knew I looked different and spoke different from the people around me. I would often get asked if I was adopted from China or Malaysia. Because I had straight hair and tan skin, I was looked upon as an outsider.

We later moved to Toronto, Ontario. The beautiful thing about Toronto is that it's so culturally diverse. I remember seeing another brown girl in my class, who had two different colored parents, and thinking that we must be similar, though I couldn't wrap my head around how we looked so physically different from one another.

The real struggle came when we moved to America. The obsession with color in America hit me like a ton of bricks. I was nine when we came to the States. We moved to the South. There was division there like I had never seen before. Certain colors of people lived in certain neighborhoods. Schools were divided.

By the time I was in tenth grade, I had attended four different schools in America. I could not go

Wellman

one day without the "What are you?" question. In the South, it's all about division and knowing your place within that division.

One day, my white friends exclaimed very proudly that they didn't have black friends. I spoke up, reminding them that I was half black. Their response was that they didn't see me as black. They said I didn't "talk black" or "dress black" or "look black," therefore I wasn't black.

That's when it hit me: I am what people see me as. I can present myself a million different ways, all true and authentic to who I am, but if someone (whether a passerby or an acquaintance) doesn't see me that way, they will change me to fit a mold that they can justify.

My experience has been nothing short of an emotional roller coaster. I've been through bouts of depression, self-loathing periods of begging to look "normal," and finally, acceptance. In my own mind, I've always just been a person. To everyone else, I'm an "other."

I identify with what I am. Black, Native, and White. I will never compromise any part of who I am in order to satisfy someone else.

Revthy Karunanith☰☰

An Indian and Chinese mix is known as a "Chindian."

So many names, so many ways of being mixed
in this vast world,
mixed itself.

The Atlantic mixes with the Pacific
and back again.

One starts to think we are only divided
because we have the names.

What is the difference between the Atlantic and the Pacific?
Are they not the same ocean?

I never really think of how the world views me racially.

Beautiful Mess.

My family came to England
before the mad rush of thousands
fleeing to the safety of the throne
of a collapsing empire,
a place promised to them
the day Britain claimed India.

But my family came from Africa.

When they arrived, few English people had ever
seen anyone like them.
My Ba told me this story as a kid:

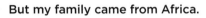

When we first got to England, they thought we were
so beautiful in our saris, and they asked us so many
questions about where we were from and about our
customs.

Then more of us came.
And then the bricks came.

Thrown through shop windows.
And then the rise of the National Front
and the Brixton Riots, which my father witnessed.

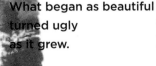

What began as beautiful
turned ugly
as it grew.

I wonder what that
says about us.

"Your culture is fine, so long as it doesn't
erode ours."

As though the mixing doesn't change all involved.
As though a chemical reaction doesn't transform
and create.

A mixing that started the day
India was made empire
and that lives today
all over the UK.

I think about my Ba and her sari
and I am proud of the mess
that we made.

mixed feelings

**Ba and Bapa Standing
in the Front Room.**

I look at this photo of my
grandparents
who stand strong and proud
in front of those who
came before them
and I feel safe
for I sense the layers of my family
peeling back through time.

And it brings
me power.

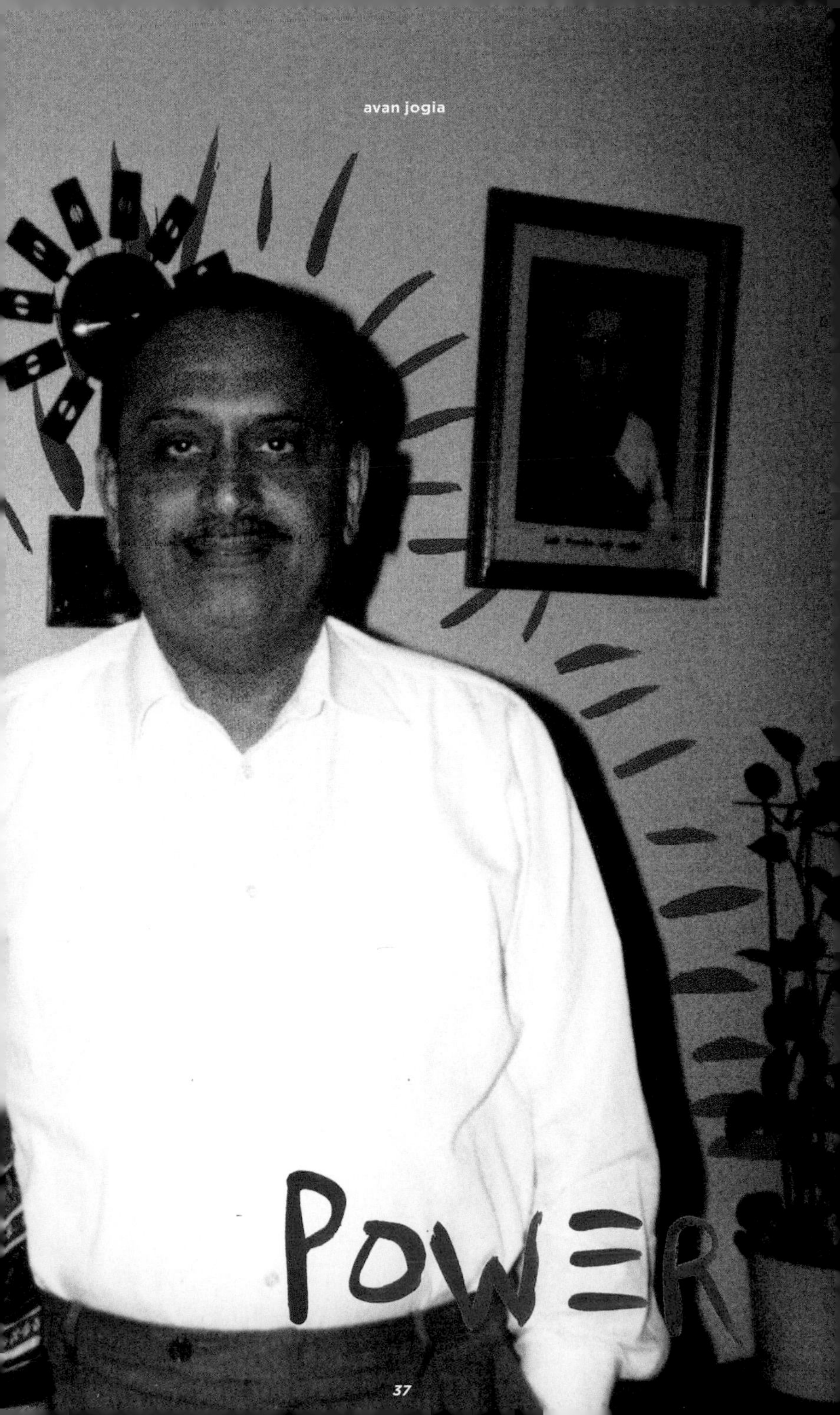
POWER

Jungle Boy

Jungle Boy.

Be wild, jungle boy,
with your hair grown past your shoulders
swinging
from tree to tree.

I want to hear you roar,
jungle boy.

Be ferocious.

Dare to scream.

Bor=d in A Boardroom.

The future is at the mercy of brutal men
with their enlarged fists bashing tables in war rooms all over
the world.
Their time passed long ago,
yet they hold on to their version of Western exceptionalism,
play the good patriot as they drop bombs on children.

They sit in their boardrooms bored by their "more." They
keep drilling and spilling and apologising and adding new
extensions to their lake homes in someplace you've never
heard of while word of prescription pills whose symptoms
include liver failure and blindness and lack of empathy fails to
get heard and out-of-court settlements settle for more while
instead leaving us less.

And they are laughing.

Yes, they cackle as our skin crackles from radiation poison
that's leaked into the water and our daughters have their
rights stripped from them and are stripped naked by fraternity
brothers on campuses that bury our children in debt and false
promises as black hands mine for coltan in the Democratic
Republic of the Congo so that I can type out this poem on my
phone and scream hysterically into the void.

Bored in a boardroom, the last lazy tycoon breathes his final
dusty breath
and as he leaves this world, beginning to burn from his greed,
we look desperately for a fire hose.

Living in between the Andre Walker
Hair Typing System.
Straight Wavy Curly Kinky
Straight Wavy Curly Kinky

Personally, I think we need
a better way to judge
or maybe never judge
a person's hair.

What makes a person who they are
can't be measured to the scale of

Straight Wavy Curly Kinky
Straight Wavy Curly Kinky

Sage Lenier

My parents didn't actually tell me I was mixed until I was eight and confused at my dad's family reunion. It was kept from me for a few reasons: One, my dad is lighter-skinned and bald, and as a kid I didn't really notice that he looked different, so I never asked. Two, my mom was slightly ashamed, and my dad refused to tell other people his race or talk about it, having been traumatized by growing up a light boy in a black family in the South. People were always asking my mom about her husband's ethnicity since I have brown skin, and she would just say, "We're Italian and she spends a lot of time outside." My dad did his best to pretend that he was white and my mom did her best to pretend that her children were white. Unpacking my racial identity was a hallmark of my teenage years. I had to do the labor of understanding what it is to be a person of color without any parental guidance or connection to the cultures my genetics hail from. I was fourteen when I stopped straightening my hair.

My grandfather's hands are strong.
They work tirelessly, fixing your watches.
My grandfather's hands are strong.
His immigrant hands
will always be fixing your watches.

He sits repairing your time,
past or present, short or long.
My grandfather's fingers are strong
and they'll always be fixing your watches.

He moves forward the arms of time
with his rusty bag of tools
and scrapes away all the grime,
polishing your metal anew.

"Your movement is broken," he says.
"That's why your clock won't tick true."

My grandfather fixes your watches,
but he doesn't do it for you.

Immigrant Song.

Cheryl Pico

Colombia is a big country. In the center, there are white Spaniards,
which is my dad, and on the coast, there are Afro-Colombians,
which is my mom. If you're fair-skinned, you're supposed to date
a fair-skinned person, and if you're dark-skinned, you're supposed
to date a fair-skinned person.

Colonialism.
Our parents of color
were told to date lighter:
a survival instinct.

But of the most unnatural kind.
To survive the wound of Colonialism.

When you are born mixed,
your grandparents pray for you:

Be light-skinned.
Have straight hair.
Have light eyes.

It's not your
Parents' fault

It's not their fault.
They were conditioned to think this way.

My parents' generation is completely oblivious. They have no idea
how much has changed and what their views have done to us.

It's not their fault.

When I got into makeup, it really changed for me. I realized that my
mother had been wearing foundation that was way too light for her.
I felt like I had to teach her. And it makes me want to cry, because
she is so beautiful. Her skin is beautiful.

American Sweethearts.

Dollar Discount David Duke
is dancing with a dark-skinned
darling named Diana.

And as they rock back and forth
to a trap arrangement of "America the Free"
they are America
and they are repulsed by each other
yet all they can do is dance
holding each other
in this emptying bar of
Rome's last day.

America is cancelled.

Science Fiction Kids

Nichelle Nichols and William Shatner shared the first
interracial kiss to be televised in US history. It was broadcast
on November 22, 1968, on the *Star Trek* episode "Plato's
Stepchildren."

It's important to note
that *Star Trek* is the only show
Brother Martin let his children watch.

It's also important to note
that *Star Trek* is what gave us
sliding doors.

Sci-fi has always been there
for people of color
and for mixed kids.

Sci-fi told me I could become an actor.

Keanu Reeves in *The Matrix*
made me think I could dodge bullets.

Turns out I can.

And so can you.

Girl/Boy.

Look
here comes the smiling boy/girl
brutal and boy-like
with bright girlish eyes
and hair that spills down
his back.

He was in love with the world
and when he'd go out to play
some parents would say,
"Look at that badly behaved little girl!"
His mum would reply,
"Actually, that's our little guy!"
The parents would smile and smugly they'd sigh,
"Then that's fine."

Look
here comes the sobbing girl/boy
casting his pearls before swine.

you ARE My
daughtER

you ARE My SON
Don't lEt thE
WORld tELL you
WhO you ARE

Sweet
couRageous
Little
onE

WHERE YOU READ YOUR FACTS AT? x

Red neck
Red hat
Where you read your facts at?

Brown skin
Brown/Black
Where you think the crown at?

Zejneb
Rauf

I am change
Made
flesh

It empowers me to think that I'm
a product of love without borders.
A breakage of barriers. A "fuck you"
to cultural norms.

I am WAR
DRUMS
BEAt!

Your blood is a brick through
the window.
Your blood is a burning riot van.
Your blood is a "fuck you" to
assumption and expectation.
Your blood is a Molotov cocktail of
bright white heat.
Your blood is a message to those
pricks in the street.

"I am change made flesh!" you can
scream.
"I am war drums beat."

Human Sculpture.

How many moments does it take to know someone?
To think you know them?
How long does it take to form them
like petty putty shaped in seconds
and cast in the flames of ignorance?
How long does it take to break that crude and silly
sculpture?
How easily can you smash it on the floor?

The Mothers.

The MothERS

My parents' mothers.
Matriarchs who made my everything.
My existence.

My Nana, who was a teenager during World War II,
was raised in an orphanage. Barnardo's home.
She hated rats because of it
and she hated porridge because of it.
Olivia Twist.
She lost a fiancé in the war,
then married my grandfather, Bud, at thirty-seven.

My Ba, who was from a wealthy Kenyan family,
was well-educated,
and before marrying my grandfather at seventeen,
wore Western dress.
And she raised her husband's siblings.
And then she raised her own kids.
And then she raised my brother and me.

When I see them together in this photograph, I smile.

What Magic ThEy
HAVE MadE.

In the third grade, I got into a

Y=s I am!

No you aren't!

*fight with a girl who did not believe me when I told her
my ethnicities. I started crying. I didn't feel I should
have to make other people believe who I am.*

Isabel
Kalogiannis

Dougla Nation.

I love you, Trini.
You have a part of my heart
in your smile.

Life lived on beaches
between doubles
and what the breeze teaches
of people
and how we sailed on ships
to shores and it reaches through
mixed pain and slavery
and evil unspeakable
speechless.

Yet the result is not weakness.
A people who are stronger because of uniqueness.
That's what Trinidad preaches.

Remember this next time you lay
on her warm golden beaches.

Bright BLUE= WARM BROWn

Growing up as a mixed kid was interesting, mainly because I grew up in Bali, which is a land full of mixed kids, so I never really felt like the odd one out or like I didn't belong.

Beautiful Bali
with your jungle heat
and ancient Hinduism
from India mixed
with Indonesia.

Gods that were familiar
to me as a child
Hanuman and Ganesha
are now beautiful crazed beings
haunting and magical and unfamiliar
having mixed with
Beautiful Bali.

The spiritual reaction of two cultures
melding into one.

Bali, like Trini,
is one of the special places.

little drummer boy

WAtch as wE Spring
up Out of thE
gRound but instEAd
of A flowER

out gRows A
CRown

Halima Khannom

I didn't really understand that my skin and background were different until the media pointed it out to me:

Don't speak Bengali too loudly in public.
Don't talk about your culture.
Pretend like you don't have one.
Do everything you need to do to show the world
that you're not a stereotypical South Asian girl.
Try to prove to them that you're one
of them.

Where are you really from?

I am born out of a collision of stars
a bright white cosmic crash
dust particles swirling since before time
sent through space on the backs of comets
and raining like a shower of life on many planets
until deciding upon this one.

Where are you really from?

I am born out of the tidal pools of the world
crawling out to greet the sun
and breathe the air
and grow fur
and hunt in packs
and paint on the walls of caves
and invent flames.

Where are you really from?

Miss Universe.

She is more than just her body
she says
But she is also her body she says

She's from Brooklyn she says
with her brown skin
with her loose Afro
she's a soul surfer
with a lip piercing

She's from Vancouver she says
with her bright green mermaid hair
with her lily-white skin
and tattooed third eye
and pet crow

She's from Los Angeles she says
with her topknot
with her sunglasses
and her Prius
and her organic diet

She's from Montreal she says
with her French words
and her long eyelashes
and her winter coat
and her little red leather gloves

She's from San Francisco she says
with her book bag
and her beautiful body hair
with her black bob
and her single-speed bike

These are all the seen things
that she is
she says

But she is also the wind she says
with her gentle breeze
and her changing weather
and her storms at times
and sometimes no wind at all

She is the sea she says
with her endless depths
with her blue-green skin
and her crashing waves at times
and sometimes her quiet stillness ·

She is the universe she says
with her cosmic consciousness
with her lack of a physical body
and her ancient mind
and her youth

She is more than what is seen
she says
She is so much more

Miss
Universe

Between "Us" and them.

You get to walk the borders between nations and cultures.

Sometimes like a tightrope-walker
walking on the edge of the cliffs between worlds.

Don't lose your balance.
Best build yourself a bridge,
little tightrope-walker.

Seems like something's got to give.
Seems like something's got to give.

Be careful,
little tightrope-walker.
I want to see you live.

Harmony harris

*People seem to have a heightened
interest in knowing my exact heritage,
and sometimes that grows from a sort
of obsession with the exotic. But their
interest can almost be used to bridge the
gap between "us" and "them."*

My Matriarchy Mantra

I was raised on the rhetoric of women who
seemed like gods to me.
They sang songs of their souls and I watched them from the
crowd, wide-eyed and enamoured.

These women raised me.

Emily Haines
Kim Gordon
Erykah Badu
Lilith
Sylvia Plath
Laura Marling
Poly Styrene
Nina Simone
Aphrodite
Kathleen Hanna
Lauryn Hill
Phoolan Devi
Artemis
and My Mother
at the center of this shrine
to holy female divine.

Mother Mary is on the crosstown as Mary Magdalene does
crosswords on the L-train to Brooklyn and Sophia the goddess of
wisdom pulls coffee in Austin and Kali is finishing her law degree
and Hera has divorced Zeus and is finding herself in Argentina as
Athena is opening her art installation at the LACMA this weekend.

Ishtar is taking a sexual studies degree at Berkeley that she'll
never use.

In the 1980s, my father moved from one big city to another: Baghdad to Belgrade (Serbia). His plan was to study engineering, and stay permanently in Serbia, as Iraq was in the midst of becoming a war zone at that time. My father became fluent in the Serbo-Croatian language and adapted very well to the European lifestyle and values.

His plans changed when the Yugoslavian war happened, and he once again had to travel to another country to seek refuge. So he ended up in Sweden, where he met a fellow refugee from the Yugoslavian war: my Bosnian mother.

The fact that they were both Muslims and could speak Serbo-Croatian made it easy for them to relate to one another and get along. In a very Muslim fashion, they got married very quickly and my mother learned to speak Arabic so that they could pass the language on to their three kids.

I grew up in the so-called Swedish "projects," which was basically where all immigrants and their children lived. Up until age eight, I only knew two people who came from an all-Swedish background. The rest of the kids at my school had roots all over the world. It's silly to say, but we didn't see each other for our ethnicities. We were all children of refugees, and therefore connected in a way.

My sister and I used to joke about us not having an identity, as we don't really feel connected to any culture one hundred percent. The Arab, Swedish, and Bosnian communities all have a strong sense of nationalism, something that I could never relate to.

I have a hard time calling myself Swedish, even though I technically am, seeing as I am a Swedish citizen and have spent my whole life here. It's still the community I feel the least attached to.

Many disregard my Bosnian side, mainly because I don't speak the language, but also because I wear a hijab. It doesn't really bug me. I choose to focus more on my history and my parents' history, rather than their nationality.

Plus, I read somewhere that in fifty years, the majority of the children who are born will be mixed kids. I'm looking forward to everyone being as ethnically disconnected and lost as I am.

Zejneb Rauf

Flowerboys.

My brother and I were raised to be flowerboys
softly swaying in the wind,
taught that men practice kindness,
taught that showing love was the most powerful thing
we could do.

Our father was a flower too.
He grew us in his garden.

Maybe one day there will be fields and fields of
flowerboys
softly swaying in the wind.
I think the world will be kinder then.
You can be a flower too.

SaMMy Sosa!

Sammy Sosa, Sammy Sosa

Skin-lightening cream used to impose an image
of how mixed people are supposed to look.

Be on the "brighter" side so you can be mistook
for looking lighter-skinned, so you don't come across as a crook.
The goal is to look a little browner, but don't you overcook.
Get out the sun.
Go get a tan.

Sammy Sosa, Sammy Sosa

Don't let them make your skin colour control you.

Sammy Sosa, Sammy Sosa

The best of us have been controlled too.

avan jogia

DREAMboy

Dreamboy.

Hello, little dreamboy.

Thinking up your future while you sleep.
I wonder who you will be.

I'd always thought that I could control my dreams
when I chose to close my eyes to sleep.
And even in waking, as I was walking,
I was dreaming up my dreams.

To see my life
laid out behind me
almost exactly as the little dreamboy dreamed
makes the cynic in me die a little +XXXXX
and the dreamboy sigh a little
as now he has more room to breathe

and dream.

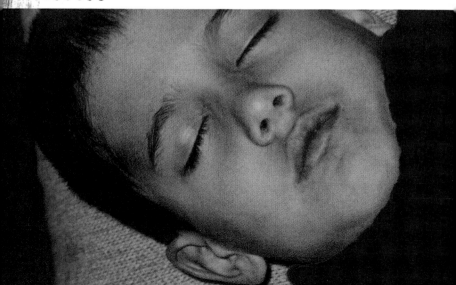

The Citizen of the World

"I have no country to fight for; my country is the earth and I am a citizen of the world."

—Eugene V. Debs

The Citizen of the World stands atop a podium
addressing the mob:

There is no country to fight for.
We are all one.
Our country is Earth,
our mother is Magma,
and our father the Sun.

RiMfatto4m

What My Parents Have.

My parents are young. Like, crazy young.
They've been together for thirty-three years, and even now,
they are in love.

Honestly? That's a lot of pressure.

I mean, look at these two. How the fuck am I supposed to
compete with that?
Am I supposed to find love like that?
That long-game love. Kids and the white picket.
Well, actually, we never had the fence.
Just a lot of bills and a Jack Russell Terrier.

In this world? Love like that?

Some people grow up without
an example of love.
Others grow up with an
unattainable example of love.

Every day loveless since
nineteen has felt like a failure.
My parents don't have the
tools to teach me about being
single in my thirties
or how to work Tinder.

I want WhAt
My PAR≡nts
hAv≡.

I want to be someone's
husband. I know that.

But not at any cost.

And They Were Fine With It?

I get insulted when people assume that my white mother's parents must've had a problem with her marrying my brown father.

I get insulted when they think her white parents are most likely racist. It furthers a stereotype about white people that I've never seen reflected in my family. I understand that it exists, but to assume it's the case is a prejudice you should maybe take a look at.

Actually, it was my father's parents who weren't down. My father's parents, who love my mother more than words can express.

That Was a

So you can miss me with that
"Your mum's white parents were fine with it?"
narrative.

It's corrosive, and it doesn't further anything.

'Cause in this case, my mother's father was so happy that his
daughter was marrying a nice man, 'cause my mother wasn't
raised nice, and my grandfather saw this nice man for what
he was: a blessing.

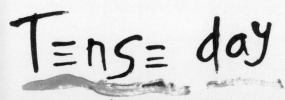

A Redenção de Cam (*The Redemption of Ham*, 1895)

BLAN quea miento

aran jogia

Blanqueamiento means whitening.
Blanqueamiento means erasure.
Blanqueamiento means whitening.
Blanqueamiento means erasure.
Blanqueamiento means whitening.
Blanqueamiento means erasure.
Blanqueamiento means whitening.
Blanqueamiento means erasure.

A Th=m= Song for Fr==_ Dom

The fireworks on Independence Day
sound like shotgun sprays
in school hallways.

This is the theme song for freedom,
and what sounds like a cheer is a scream
and the strings are the yelling of children
and the drumline is an AR-15.

This is the theme song for freedom
but I fear that it falls on deaf ears
because they say when you're shooting a gun,
freedom is impossible to hear.

Mother Told Me.

Mother told me

Make light
to make light.
Don't take it too seriously, my
little one.
You'll grow up to think too much.
Just stay soft and you'll be
strong.

Mother told me

Make light
to make love.
Don't be so serious, my little one.
Don't be so afraid of loss
because loss happens to
everyone.

Mother told me

Make light
to make life.
Life's not that serious, my little
one.
Keep your chin above the dark
because life happens to
everyone.

Lucie Lalarme

When I went to the USA, on one of the forms, there was a question about race, but "mixed" wasn't an option. I had to tick the one that said that I was black. (I'm pretty sure I would have been in trouble if I had put both white and black, because that's not how they see me.)

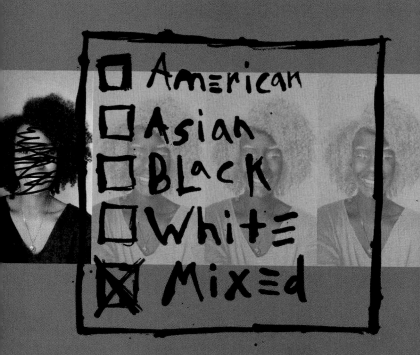

☐ American
☐ Asian
☐ Black
☐ White
☒ Mixed

I am standing in Immigration.
I am sixteen years old.
It's fucking boiling.
There is a family in front of me arguing,
and it is my first time to the States.

For reasons both known and unknown to me, I am terrified.

The reasons known to me are these:

I am about to test for my first television show. Just a Canadian kid,
precocious and post-conscious. The show is a FOX pilot where I
play the Indian sidekick to an "older white guy with an acerbic wit
but a heart of gold." (This was the description of every lead part,
in every pilot, on every network that year. *House* was coming to
a close and they were all trying to collect, I guess.) Regardless, I
am over the moon to play the side-bit Indian, funny man, ha ha ha,
look at him he doesn't know anything. Boy's gotta eat.

And times were different.

I am standing in a line that swirls and spins for miles, it seems.
I'm standing with my mother, who has quit her job cutting hair to
help me
put on makeup and say other people's words, god bless her.

So we are standing, and we are filling out a form.

And this is what we see.
And I realise that I am not on this list.
And I realise, as I fly to play out an Indian stereotype,
that there is no form for me.

What forms me
doesn't get a box.

R=sting in Prid=

I'm physical evidence that love is more than just skin colour. I'm my ancestors' wildest dreams. I'm the fear of every racist. I am history, I am present, I am future. I am valid and enough, regardless of what naysayers might say. I don't have to pick sides. I'm two, made into one. I'm proof that borders are just imaginary lines made to separate people. I'm anarchy, in my own way, rebellion against the norm.

R=sting in PoW=R

I am my ancestors' wildest dreams,
their many souls spinning on the
wheel
all with different faces
or without faces.
Instead a flower.
I am my ancestors' wildest dreams.

Resting in pride.

Resting in power.

Karinn=
Mahé

MIXED RACE Culture is

I identify as black. It's hard to identify as mixed-race because it feels like a paper-thin category. I don't know of any mixed-race culture (Key and Peele?). It's so broad, it could mean anything.

"It's so broad, it could mean anything" is the point of this whole exercise.
"It's so broad, it could mean anything" is the path forward.

Mixed-Race Culture is _____
Mixed-Race Culture is _____
Mixed-Race Culture is _____
Mixed-Race Culture is _____
Mixed-Race Culture is _____
Mixed-Race Culture is _____

and Mixed-Race Culture is *Key and Peele*, of course.

Nour Djilane

I've recently discovered that we are the glue. We are the bond, the adhesive, the cement in the middle. We fill the cracks in our foundation. We bring seemingly unmovable forces together. Who would have thought that a child could move continents? We blend cultures the way we blend families, through time and through love.

We Put Shit together.

J≡SS Gianatasio

WE the GLU∃

us first
us first

Family Connections.

He is your Ba's sister's first daughter's kid. Chetan!

My father will sit and explain our family connections to you for longer then you are willing to hear about it. Most of the time, he will be wrong in some way and he will tell you this like you should have known the whole time.

My father loves his family and he will always put them first. Us first.

It's something that's rubbed off on me, even though I don't know all the connections, and so I ask all the questions, and try to memorise all the extensions of my ever-growing family tree.

You know! She is Bhavin's brother's eldest auntie.

Harlaj Kaur

This summer, my cousin, who is also Punjabi, will be marrying a half white and half Vietnamese girl.

I have a picture of my mother in a sari that I think is beautiful.
It's from her wedding day.

In it,
her face is turned down and her hair is bright blonde.
(She was a hairdresser so it was different every week.)
Her hands are covered in henna
and she's wearing bangles and earrings of gold.
She looks serene and happy.
And I can feel my father in the room.
And all of my father's family
guiding her through the steps of an Indian wedding.
To me she looks as if she is exactly where she is meant to be.
Starting her life with her husband, my father.

When I asked if that photo could be included in this book she replied:

"No, dear, I'd hate for people to think I am culturally appropriating anything."

The news of them dating wasn't as shocking to the younger people of the family as it was to some of the older ones. They didn't take it too hard, but it did take a bit of time for a few of them to adjust. Now we're all just waiting until next week, when their wedding day will come, and we will have a new member in our family.

avan jogia

Children are cruel. They pick out difference as weakness.

"Dot or Feather?"
is what I used to get a lot
when I would tell kids in my class
about my father's Indian bloodline.

How the fuck you gonna reduce
their culture and mine
to "Dot or Feather?"

"Sitting Indian"
"Indian Summer"
"Indian Giver"

Scot McMaster

I'm not your fucking "Dot or Feather"
the two together.
Difference people misnamed,
colonial blood shamed.
Boats boarding beaches
and lands claimed.

And who's blamed?
Not me.

I'm not your fucking
"Dot or Feather."

Growing up as a mixed person, I felt sort of lost. There were times when I wished I was only Kenyan or only Lao so I could feel closer to either side of my family.

Just to have the peace of not being comprised of pieces. To have your simplicity. To feel as one. Instead of no one.

Just to have the
PEACE of not
being
comprised
of Pieces

I felt uncomfortable a lot because people didn't understand how I could be Asian and black. My classmates thought I was only black, and I guess they did not understand the concept of being mixed.

Just to have the peace of not being comprised of pieces. They make you one. You're _____ . That's easier.

Kwamboka
Ndege

I suppose I identify mainly as black due to how I look. But I still acknowledge my Lao side and love that it's half of me, even if some people don't notice.

Just to have the peace of not being comprised of pieces.

I grew up in a super multicultural community where the majority were Greek, Vietnamese, and indigenous Australians. Being of mixed race really helped me identify with each of those cultures.

Joshua Griffin

The SυpⲢⲢ PowⲢrs of being Mix≡d

The superpowers of being mixed.
The understanding of everyone.
The ability to see both sides.
All sides.
No sides.

To see the world as it coincides with another
and each other as we whirl and swirl on our mother, Earth.

The superpowers of being mixed
are bestowed upon you at your birth.

I do believe the current discourse is spreading an awareness of race as a spectrum, but it's still so ignorant in many ways. I'd say that the world views me as a particularly exotic specimen, which I take as a great compliment.

subtle things

There's no rule book on how to
raise the mixed race children
and, as such, I would never
label my parents as ignorant. I
am eternally grateful to them
for the upbringing I received.
I've found, however, that as
I've grown older and become
more socially aware, that there
are multiple aspects of my life
that they will never understand
as single-race individuals.

Carlos Gurnani

My Mother's Father's Bowie Knife.

My mother gave me her father's Bowie knife
'cause I liked sharp things and *Aladdin Sane*.
Her father was a farmer
or a plastic factory worker
or an inventor
or an aviator
or a small-town genius with dyslexia.

My grandfather was the man who told my mother to look up
at stars and suns and taught her their many names.

And for me, my mother did the same.

Christmas '95.

Christmas was the only holiday my mother cared to celebrate.

I was culturally raised in my father's family
and the only thing that stayed
was Christmas.

Christmas!

Not religious.
Just something that they could give us.

And even though we were broke
We still got gifts 'cause we were good kids.

Anyway, Christmas Day.
We would open presents one by one to make the moment last.
Now, either present or past, I try and make good moments last.

I look back at all the effort that was made.
I'm reminded when I look at this photo,
as my memories start to fade,
that I am just a product of the foundation that was laid.

Neighbourhood Kids.

Me and the neighbourhood kids who
grew up in The Gardens
catching grass snakes and playing
Pokémon cards and
we were all the same age.

We would be let out in the morning
and we wouldn't come home till the sun
went away
and we knew everyone's mother.

They yelled at us like they birthed us.
Sneaking undercover.
And everything was beautiful and safe
at that innocent age.

Me and the neighbourhood kids who
grew out of The Gardens.
Some of us hardened,
some started to darken,
but I had it luckier I guess.

My parents stayed together.
Mortgage stress
to change our address
and I'm blessed.

Me and the neighbourhood kids plucked
out of The Gardens.
Still there grow a hundred seeds.
Still there grow a hundred me's.

Laser Tag '99.

Our neighbourhood looked like the United Nations.
Everyone with different faces.

I worry about kids who grow up in mono-racial communities
seeing only themselves reflected back at them.
Seeing only their own problems reflected back at them.

Young eyes need to see all sides
to construct a real worldview.
I grew up with the poor and the rich,
all kinds of kids.

If everybody looks like you, then run.
And find somewhere new.

THEN RUN!

CARPET*

My grandparents' carpet.

Bangles on the Nightstand.

I am spending the weekend at my grandmother's house.
My grandfather lives here too, but make no mistake:
this is my grandmother's house.

This is what the lights look like in my grandmother's house.
They are bright blue-white.
She has changed over to the new lightbulbs
to save money
and her house looks like a Costco
bathed in bright blue-white.

This is what the kitchen looks like in my grandmother's
house.
The fridge is from '87 and the pots are from '64.
She has a pan from Africa that's in the bottom drawer
and it smells of oil and incense.
And she has left a plate of pears out
to be eaten by my grandfather as he passes through.

This is what the living room looks like in my grandmother's
house.
My grandfather has cricket on.
It's been on for five days and no one knows the score.
There are fabric sleeves on the couch armrests,
their purpose still a mystery to me.
Krishna and Ganesh and Hanuman are watching as India
beats South Africa 1245 wickets to 603
and my grandmother has moved the pear plate to the
living room
and my grandfather cheers and eats.

This is what the bedroom looks like in my grandmother's
house.
I never spent much time here as a child, but now, as an adult,
I see the small revealing secrets of a room I used to think
was so boring.
Like the nightstand where she leaves her bangles and
necklace.
There is something so regal about it.
She has much honour, my grandmother, and pride,
and strength,
with her bangles on the nightstand.

mixed feelings

TIMES
WATCHMAK

The family Shop in

South London

Saminah Manshi

Half + half does not equal a whole.

Oh, but it does.
I know it can feel like it doesn't sometimes
but know this:
You are whole.
As whole as the land and the ocean make the earth.

as whole as the
Sun and Moon
Make the
Earth

*My dad would go to the same Thai restaurant in Hollywood
and order the same thing every single time. It got to the
point where as soon as he walked in, the waitress would
immediately bring out his order. The waitress was my mom.*

I went into the restaurant to see you
and sat at my usual table.
And sat in my usual chair. And was unusually sad.

You weren't working yet,
and I was sure I had your shifts down right.
I ordered something light.
It came out and it was fine.
But I guess the food tastes different when
you aren't here to serve it.
Quite nervous when I put my order through,
not sure if I deserved it,
to talk to you.

I went into the restaurant to see you
and sat at my usual table.
And sat in my usual chair.
And you were there,
standing with a ribbon in your hair.
Taking orders from the customers.
I'll wait my turn to talk to you.
I wouldn't dare to call you over.
I'll wait my turn to talk to you.

I went into the restaurant to see you
and you were only ten minutes late.

I went into the restaurant to see you.
A suitable place, I felt, for our first date.

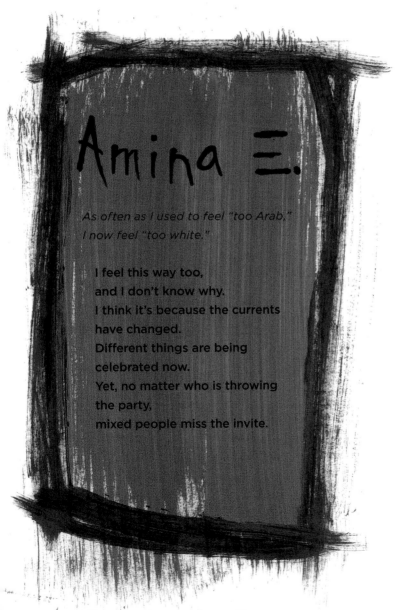

Amina E.

As often as I used to feel "too Arab,"
I now feel "too white."

I feel this way too,
and I don't know why.
I think it's because the currents
have changed.
Different things are being
celebrated now.
Yet, no matter who is throwing
the party,
mixed people miss the invite.

We Might Be Mixed.

I might be mixed
but I am not half of anything.
I'm a full being.

I might be mixed
but I am not starved for anything.
I'm a full being.

Fruit from two trees nourishes me.
I might be different from you, although slightly.
But like me,
you perceive differently.

You see with different sight.
Please remember to add sound to your sight.
We need the shine from your light.
We need less bark and more bite.

You might be mixed
but you're not half of anything.
You're a full being.

The world deserves to
see your sight.
Your point of view makes
us full-seeing.

I AM Not Half of Anything I AM a full BEING

I'm mixed, but I am extremely light-skinned, to the point that people don't believe me when I say my dad is black. Due to this, I think I was able to dodge a world of hateful comments. Some might say that this is a blessing, and I guess it kind of is. I've had people tell me before that I "don't count" as being mixed, and I sometimes tell myself that I "don't count" either. Obviously, I know this isn't true, but that doesn't make it any easier to feel unseen.

People just want to be seen.

When you say we lack the melanin to be mixed,
that's erasure.

Pick pick pick away
at our already confused identity.
Pick pick pick away.

Miranda Patterson

We can't say people "don't count."
Don't count? In what?
In the larger scale of who is white and who is brown?
Who is keeping score of this thing?
For me personally, that's all just sound.
And it doesn't help me as I try to ground
who I am.

Pick pick pick away
at our already confused identity.
Pick pick pick away.

People just want to be seen.

And it's completely a mind game. Parts of me think I can't do x, y, and z because of how light I am.

avan jogia

Look at all Workers

I would like to provide my first memory of insecurity concerning my ethnicity. I'm not sure how this memory was conceived, but I knew that my mom worked graveyard shifts at the hospital. I remember her coming home, parking the car in the front yard because she had fallen asleep on the way home. Some days she wouldn't even come in the house. So this is the first memory: a white woman, with pearls on, a polka-dot dress, and an apron coming down a staircase. I am standing in the doorway and she welcomes me with a smile. This woman, instead of my mom, represented what I thought financial security was. What an easy way of life looked like. I was too young to understand what I was feeling but I knew it was wrong, and that I was at some sort of . . . It's hard to express in words the emotions I recall and still feel when I think about this. I don't even know why she looked like she was from the '50s. Anyways.

Isabella Rivera

mixed feelings

The Mixed Person's Prayer.

At first, there is no light within you
and the gods
in all their colours and shades cry out:

Be YOU
for in your YOU-ness
we are there
howling around you
like a storm of your own certainty.

Having heard their words,
the light within you flickers alive and asks
What if ME isn't enough?

And the gods reply:
You have all of us within you.
Shiva, in their infinite forms,
Athena, in their infinite wisdom,
Hachiman, in their infinite strength,
Oko, in their infinite growth,
Ra, in their infinite light,
and all those named and unnamed
gods of your ancestors.

Be YOU
for in your YOU-ness
we are there
howling around you
like a storm of your own certainty.

My Mother.

I see now how brave you were, to stand there, marrying
the person you love, the person you've been with now for
thirty-plus years. The person you have children with.

My father's father,
my bapa,
our patriarch.
He wasn't going to come to the wedding.
As you sat waiting in your sari.
The same bapa
who loves you so dearly,
who held me as a child,
who loves me so dearly.

Thank you for being brave.

Thank you for holding out through the judgment.

Thank you for creating this temple,
this family,
for us.

I love you.

My Father.

I see now how brave you were, to stand there, marrying
the person you love, the person you've been with now
for thirty-plus years. The person you have children with.

How brave you were to say,
"This is the woman I love," staring at her in your suit.
The first person in our family
to marry outside of the culture,
you were a path forward for many.
You built that path and made us.

Thank you for being brave.
Thank you for holding out through the judgment.

Thank you for creating this temple,
this family,
for us.

I love you.

My father

Aida Fadiogi

*I don't look European, so I was never mistaken for a tourist
when I was walking in Casablanca. However, when I was a child
and I was outside with my mom, who is light-skinned and has
green eyes, people would give us confused looks, or they would
suppose I was her maid.*

I promise that's my mother.
I promise you that I am her daughter,
not her maid.

*Nearly every time at the airport, when I was going to visit my
family in Belgium, customs officers would ask me if she really
was my mom and if my dad knew we were leaving the country.*

Personally, I never had a family trip
that didn't include my dad going through a separate line.

Me, my mother, and my brother learned to laugh.

Laughter, it seemed, was the best way to hide.
And it wasn't until I was older that it
happened to me.
I was pulled into the separate line.

Finally old enough to be a threat,
I walk through customs cautiously now.
Just waiting to be pulled aside.

I guess everyone just sees me as foreign.

TSA VIP.

My brother looks like
bargain-bin bin Laden
and the TSA agrees.

They pull us out of the line
into the VIP
into the fucking VIP
where we get the special
treatment
where they graze our
bodies with the backs
of their hands.

So exclusive. So VIP.
Very Inspected People
in the VIP.

Then you're in

A little louder for the people in the back:
Let's reframe how we see the world.
We like categories, as humans,
so let's just broaden the requirements.
Do you breathe air?
Check.
Bleed red?
Check.
Want love?
Check.

Then you're in.

MEL QuaN

When I was younger, I was living in Brasil and went to a public school there. I experienced racism for, I think, the first and only time there.

Racism isn't American.
Racism isn't American.
Racism isn't American.

And so, to my Americans:
Change the way you see yourself as a nation
and maybe you will be able to change your behaviour.
How you see yourself is your saviour.
Like an addict,
you must forgive yourself and
tomorrow be braver.
Racism isn't American.
So tomorrow be braver.

Racism isn't American.
So tomorrow be braver.

I didn't experience racism in the United States. I lived in Hawaii where I also attended public schools. Hawaii is so incredibly diverse, I never had someone mock me for anything related to my race or ethnicity.

Racism isn't American
So tomorrow b= braver

Thick Skin Mixed Skin

Thick skin.
As thick as the skin that I'm in.
Mixed skin.
Mixed in with whatever's within.

'Cause it was dang=Rous to b= BROWN Aft=R 2001

I tried to soften my father's bloodline.
To change my brown to something that was less threatening.
It breaks my heart to think of it now,
that I would ever do something to erase him from myself.

No, that will never do.

I'm sorry, Papa.

I'm very proud of you.

A Boy and
his fath=R

Pops.

Let Sleeping Racists Die.

Nico from the Velvet Underground
was a vicious racist.
She stuck a mixed girl in the eye with
a wine glass screaming,
"I hate black people!"

Think about that.
And people still fuck with her.
I don't have that sort of privilege.
The privilege to ignore who she is
because
"she has such a vibe."

The fuck outta here.
All she did is sing "The Jew."
Lou's songs.

"Every once in a while, there'd be
something about Jews and I'd be,
'But Nico, I'm Jewish,' and she was like
'Yes, yes, I don't mean you.'"*

Fuck Nico.
She ain't that cool.
Let sleeping racists die.

Asiah Accola

I refused to go outside to keep my skin pale.

Dance, little one,
in rays of sun.
Let your skin darken with her power.
Don't turn and twist from her embrace.
I know you are hurting.
I know why you shy away to shade.
To hide away your face.

Let her hold your body
and see what her love creates.
Let her colour your skin with her paintbrush,
little one, and see what can be made
when you live in the sun
and out of the shade.

LEXi KLEiSS

In February 2018, following the release of Black Panther, I finally realised what it means to be a person of colour and to be proud of my ethnicity. It dawned on me that I should take pride in being different, that I should embrace my life as someone whose history exemplifies strength and encourages and embraces a strong culture. Since then, I introduce myself as a mixed-race person without identifying myself directly as one or the other: I am a melting pot of races and cultures that have accumulated in my bloodline.

Black Panther, roar for your culture.
Bengal Tiger, roar for your culture.
Proud Lion, roar for your culture.

Bengali Tiger

Mask Maker.

I am, above all things, a mask
maker.
This is the function I perform
more than any other.
I breathe better with a mask on.
Like an oxygen mask
pumping my identity into my
lungs.

I am a mask maker.
I build them out of wood and stone,
sometimes out of friends or deities.
I disassemble my idols and use their bones and hair to glue
together a freakish identity of my own creation.
A shamanistic ritual of bloodletting icons and historical
figures,
authors and poets,
actors and rock stars.
I use every part of the animal in my masks,
and like the hunter, I waste nothing.
Every gesture, observed and devoured.

I am a maker of masks. You like my mask.
You say it suits me
even though you can see my Elvis Presley snarl
and my Montgomery Clift eyes.
Even though you can tell I hold my pen like Baudelaire,
you entertain my pretense.
You enjoy my fantasy.
What is life without it?

Bowie
Cave

I am, above all things, a mask maker.
But now the glue has settled and stuck
and I pull at my cheeks as my skin starts to tear.
And now there is just a black hole where my face used to be.
Until I make my next mask,
who knows who I'll be.

Buddha
christ
Krishna

My Uncles.

I remember looking up to all of you,
my uncles, my kakas.
I remember how you dressed.
Snappy dressers, the men in my family.
Famously late for everything because
getting ready took so long.
Green Gucci bottle cologne
and shiny pointed shoes.
It's probably where I get my flare from.

The uncle in this photo isn't here anymore.
I used to swing from his arms.
He was the glue.
Everyone looked up to him.
The family
hung its hopes on him.

I want to get all of my kakas
together again.
It's been years, I think,
but it's the fear, I think,
that the room might feel
one seat empty.

But Amit would love it. I know it.
And once we got some rum and cokes flowing,
well, maybe there is no way of knowing.
Just trying to mend a broken stitch
with some sewing.

Tailoring a moment with my kakas.

For Security Reasons

These guys need to come up with new lines.
We aren't fucking buying it.

Racism masquerading as "A Concern for Safety" is one of
the oldest and, by far, most transparent of the Ten Fascist
Commandments.

They are as follows:

1. Racism by Way of Security
2. Nationalism to the Point of Deity
3. Supremacy by Way of the Military
4. Sexism as a Tool of Suppression
5. Censorship as a Tool of Suppression
6. Fear as a Tool of Suppression
7. Corporate Interests Protected
8. Labourer Interests Ignored
9. Cronyism in Place of Professionalism
10. Disdain for Intellectuals and the Arts

Now look at your leaders,
and try not to explode with rage.

My parents met in Dallas, Texas. My father emigrated from Pakistan to Texas in the 1980s. My parents initially met in a gay bar in the queer-friendly part of Dallas. Soon after, they properly met and spoke to each other when my father discovered my mom at her retail job in an Army Navy Surplus store. They dated for a while, and my mother was already learning about and involving herself with Islam at her local mosque and her college's Muslim Student Alliance. She accepted Islam on her own, and then married my father. People tend to assume she was forced to convert in order to marry my father, and my mother is always proud to correct that assumption.

Saalika Khan

Nice.

The thing about it is, it's nice.

This beach town where the cops have bottle openers
on their utility belts instead of handcuffs
and the mothers cluck and cluck and turn their heads
like hens
and the kids drink too much and fall off the boardwalk.

The thing about it is, it *is* nice.

Everyone says good morning until 11:59 AM
and then, a minute later, they only say goodnight
and at the baseball field a bunch of pimple-faced
16-year-old girls
are playing softball and everyone watches as they drink
from tin cans of piss-water beer with "America"
written on the side.

The thing about them is, they're nice.

With their tight-lipped smiles, stretching, strained,
like Christians laughing at a sex joke.
They know it's funny, but they also know their god
is watching them laugh.
And the beaches are beautiful and the water is warm
and the drinks are cold and the responsibility is none
and the sense of consequence is minimal.

The thing about it is, you can leave here feeling dirty.

Like you've just preformed a perverse time-traveling act.
Like it was all a '50s fever dream without the racists and the
misogynists.

Well, that's the idea.
Then the men start talking down to the women
and the women all smile and apologise for their husbands.

That's the idea.
Then a group of linen-shirted hounds chant "Paki" at you
outside their parents' yacht club.

That's the idea.
Till you realise you're the only brown face for miles and miles
of beautiful white sand beach.

The thing about it is, I like it.

It's a conflict, and I'm not sure why.
Sure, they are all delusional, but so is everyone.
Isn't that the point?
To find some small pocket of delusion
when confronted with constant and unwavering reality?
Isn't that what I do when I write?

Anyway.
I'm at the baseball field
and its the bottom of the 9th,
and I've got my "America" beer
and I'll happily explain to you
the ethnic origin of my name.

My complexion is complex

My complexion is complex.

Have to look back at my blood for some context.
My bloodline is part of what's on next.
Old text, seemingly written down like a reflex.

My complexion is honey-brown.
I can't believe I'm what's coming now
when before I felt that if I were just a little less caramel
I could be comparable
to something more air-able.

My complexion is sand-gold.
The soul feels new, but the hands old.
The path forward is hard, yet it's handled.

Do it for the art,
power structure dismantled.
Just say what's in your heart,
given a chance with the mantle.

My complexion is complex.

CLEANing up AftER you

We stand right beside you as you say things
we can't stand for.
You don't see us
as you insult our mothers
and fathers.

We stand right beside you as you say things
we can't stand for.
I wonder how many of us speak up?
They're hard, your words, your "jokes," your throwaway
remarks. Why is it my job to come clean up after you?

You created this.
This unnatural moment
that I must untwist.
It's inconvenient, but here I am,
untwisting your words, cleaning up after you,
because I can't bear my own silence.

I will not swallow your poison.
I refuse to show my anger
only in my eyes.

The Bag of Motivations.

Everybody's bound to their bag of motivations spilling out
across the table.
Try to see them if you're able.
No more separate sides.
No more Cain and Abel.

This bag of motivations is woven with fabric of the soul.
Also with where the soul was raised
and by whom.
The contents of the bag are pieces of you.
Bits and bobs built over time and discovery.

But the bag isn't you.

So when you are influenced by your bag, remember:
You can simply put it down.
It's your bag, not the other way around.

But the bag Isnt you !

Growing up with mixed heritage was complicated because of my parents' divorce. There was a part of each of them that hated the other's culture, yet that culture was also a part of my identity. My father would hate the stereotypical Brazilian carefree spirit, my mother would hate the supposed rigidity of Indian culture.

It seems when there is strife,
we concentrate on what makes us different
rather than what makes us whole.
What divides us
rather than what's inside us.
We reduce ourselves to old rhetoric,
blame their blood for their inability to love
or their heritage, their religion, their race, or their
parentage. Blame what they're made of
rather than face the unfortunate truth
that all your love
and all their effort
just wasn't enough.

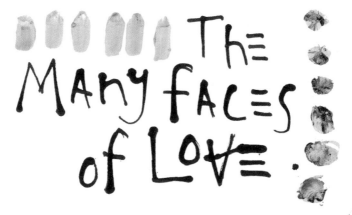

Mixed Drinks

A murky bar of familiar faceless patrons
drinking "mixed" cocktails.
2 parts segregation.
1 part solitude.
To the daughters and sons of the world:
I'll share a drink with all of you.
Come raise a glass to how we feel,
come share a cup of gratitude.

Th= eye can't
S== all of m=

The eye can't see all that is there.
For underneath this silly skin I wear
is a world of thought
and spirit.

For underneath my fabled family tree
are buried roots strong and out of sight.

The eye can only see my skin.
Unseeable, my sacred soul within.

One day the eye might scratch below the
surface.

Wolf cubs.

Community Pool Summer of '98

I am the little boy who stands
in the pool alone with my hands
in the water,
thinking too hard to play.

And when I emerge from the pool, I weep for
my pruning hands.

This is the
day I L≡arned
to ride A Bik≡

The Kids Aren't All White.

The kids aren't all white
as they reach out of the basement
tired by now of patience
rising up to meet the rising sun
the new-dawn-green-lawn-brown-picket-fence
sort of existence
born out of persistence
and resistance
pistons pump the engine on
consistent
as they dare to jump
to shine their light on
bare pawns
unable to see what's going on
swan song
to the days that seem long gone
bye to
the wrong of the gone era
death of the past
we're the pallbearers organised and angry young Che Guevara
as we crawl out of the basement
faced with what's really been going on
still the power is strong
gripped tight the fist
and the lights are on
fight night 'cause our rights are gone
fist smite 'cause our might is long
King Kong
top of the tower
late is the hour
bang the goddamn gong

The Kids Ar=n't
all Whit≡

the kids aren't all white
and that's all right

sing long the rising song

Acknowledgments.

I would like to say thank you to all of you who have contributed your stories to this book. Who wrote me thousands of letters. There would be no book without all of you. Your honesty about your experiences inspired me daily, and I'm happy to have had your support. This book is for you. Thank you.

To my family, I love you. Thank you for making up my parts. I feel that fullness every day.

To Cleopatra, I love you.

Andrews McMeel Publishing
a division of Andrews McMeel Universal
1130 Walnut Street, Kansas City, Missouri 64106

www.andrewsmcmeel.com

19 20 21 22 23 RR2 10 9 8 7 6 5 4 3 2 1

ISBN: 978-1-4494-9621-0

Library of Congress Control Number: 2019939322

Background images © Getty Images pages 14, 28-29, 59-60, 72-73, 92-93, and 106-107.

Page 72: *The Redemption of Ham*, Modesto Brocos, Wikimedia Commons, public domain.

Page 112: Fields, Danny. "From the Velvets to the void." By Simon Reynolds. The Guardian, 16 Mar 2007. https://www.theguardian.com/music/2007/mar/16/popandrock3

ATTENTION: SCHOOLS AND BUSINESSES
Andrews McMeel books are available at quantity discounts with bulk purchase for educational, business, or sales promotional use. For information, please e-mail the Andrews McMeel Publishing Special Sales Department: specialsales@amuniversal.com.